IF YOU THINK YOU'VE GOT IT ROUGH . . .

then say hello to Herman. His kid likes to roll down windows in the automatic car wash. His dentist is overzealous with the drill. And his wife would never win the Miss Congeniality competition. But Herman's hanging in there, giving you a laugh on every page.

⊘

More Big Laughs from SIGNET

HERMAN

"In one of your moods again, Herman?"

by
JIM UNGER

A SIGNET BOOK
NEW AMERICAN LIBRARY

Published by arrangement with Andrews, McMeel & Parker

The cartoons in *In One of Your Moods Again, Herman?*
appeared originally in *The 1st Treasury of Herman*

"Herman" is syndicated internationally by
UNIVERSAL PRESS SYNDICATE

SIGNET TRADEMARK REG. U.S. PAT. OFF. AND FOREIGN COUNTRIES
REGISTERED TRADEMARK—MARCA REGISTRADA
HECHO EN CHICAGO, U.S.A.

SIGNET, SIGNET CLASSIC, MENTOR, PLUME, MERIDIAN, AND
NAL BOOKS are published by New American Library,
1633 Broadway, New York, New York 10019

First Signet Printing, March, 1985

1 2 3 4 5 6 7 8 9

PRINTED IN THE UNITED STATES OF AMERICA

"I can't explain now, but don't take your jacket off at work."

"I plugged it in to see if you'd fixed it."

"D'you get the feeling one of us is getting
ripped-off?"

"I called earlier but your wife said you hadn't got the brains to read these books."

"Oh goody! You found my comb."

"I know I'm scraping the barrel, but d'yer
wanna dance?"

"This idiot opened all the windows halfway through the car wash."

"Keep in mind you're a guest on this bench."

"I don't think I'll bother with a tan 'til I get out."

"I can't see any sense in this! We passed about 10 fish markets on the way here."

"And in recognition of your 20 years loyal service
in the X-ray department..."

"I know it's your first time in 38 years, but what would happen if everyone was ten minutes late for work?"

"The art teacher told us not to get disheartened
if our first portrait looked like a hippopotamus
with a hat on."

"Columbus, will yer sit down and stop
asking all these dumb questions?"

"What did you spoil his tiger trap for...?"

"The bank wants to lend us five thousand bucks
to get out of debt!"

"Whadyer mean you wanna marry my daughter
... I thought you were my daughter!"

"You'd better stay off solid food for an hour or two."

"Keep going! I'll run out and mortgage the house and meet you at the check-out."

'Wake up! Marcus Welby here is trying to saw off your leg.'

"You wait! As soon as someone discovers
gravity, they'll all come down and hit the ground."

"I'm sure you'll agree, we don't want an epidemic."

"Did you shake the bottle?"

"They wouldn't let people stand here if it was dangerous."

"Pretend you're a purse snatcher, I wanna
try something."

"Have you got a window-seat?"

"Look what your stupid uncle gave us. What
d'yer think it is?"

"Next time you go to the store, get some proper paper napkins."

"Ignore him. He knows he's due for his
annual shots."

"Four months, eight days, five hours and twenty minutes. Four months, eight days, five hours and nineteen minutes."

"The paper's okay and the ink's okay. You left the 'w' out of 'twenty'!"

"It'll take you a couple of days to get used to
these express elevators."

"Whaddyer mean, 'Which one is ours?'"

"I hope you never need a brain transplant. It'll be rejected."

"Okay, Racquel, but what are you gonna
tell my wife?"

"If you were a horse we could have shot yer!"

"In two days I'll owe $3,000.00 on a library book
I haven't even read."

"If you're gonna stay like that all weekend, I think you'd better start smoking again."

"What's a good hand signal for backing onto a freeway?"

"Every time we go out anywhere, you always find something to complain about."

"Take it easy, take it easy. I've come to fix the window."

"I got fantastic references from my last five jobs but I lost them on the way over here."

"There, you leave your toys all over the floor
and now Mommy can't watch her
favorite program."

"His teacher wants you to bake a cake for him to take to school. Must be a geology lesson."

"Going up the Amazon?"

"That's it, perfect . . . keep it there."

"How would you like to eat off the floor
every day?"

"Don't forget it's my mother's
birthday tomorrow."

"You've got six wives waiting for you on the outside. Are you sure you want a parole?"

"Writing your autobiography! Who's it about?"

"I thought T.V. was supposed to make
you violent!"

"Tomorrow morning I'm having you adopted."

"Watch out...the plate's hot."

"Don't blame me. I was cleaning his cage and he
flew up the pipe."

"Hold still! I dropped my little mirror."

"I can do shorthand! It just takes a little longer."

"Are you sure you're comfortable?"

"Is this your first blind date?"

"Smarten up! Sometimes I think your father's got
more brains than you have."

"I don't wanna be a juror! Can't I be
a witness?"

"Me and the boys were trying to guess how
you spell your name."

"How does it feel to take some little kid's last fifteen cents in the whole world?"

"If you keep bugging me about getting married,
I'm gonna break off our engagement."

"Why don't you listen. I said you need a
chiropractor not choir practice!"

"If I have to keep going to school, all the best jobs are gonna be snapped up."

"I'm not sneering at your qualifications. I just wasn't aware you could get a B.A. for 'flower arrangement!'"

"HERMAN...did you forget to water my plants while I was away?"

"I thought while I was getting the fuses, I'd pick up a few groceries."

"Mom said we can get married and live in the
dining room if you don't mind eating
in the kitchen."

"That's a relief. I thought I'd gone deaf!"

"A car or boat, maybe; but I'm not lending you
money for food."

"We are now joining our regularly scheduled commercials which are already in progress."

"Have a good vacation. I've decided not to give you your bad news until you get back."

"This t.v. dinner's got wires in it!"

"You dropped it. You get it!"

"That's just his way of saying he wants you to stay!"

"...and don't call me illiterate. My Ma and Pa
have been married for thirty-eight years."

"Look in my sister's blue bag."

"He wouldn't eat it so I put in some dirt and
made it look like mud."

"You can't be expected to get it right first time!"

"Why don't you buy a proper set of headphones?"

"I wanted to leave you a tip but I haven't got change for a quarter."

"Teacher says if I don't do well at school, I'll end up like you."

"I know your landlord depends on the rent but you still can't list him as a dependent."

"Saturday evenings with you are a real treat."

"Here, don't touch the stick."

"It'll take you a couple of days to get used to them."

SCHOOL OF KARATE

"We're not gonna charge you for this first lesson."

"He's getting better. He can remember everything
now except getting married."

"I was gonna give you fresh garden peas but I couldn't find the can opener."